THE AWESOME
3-D ART
COLORING GUIDE

LEARN 3-D COLORING TECHNIQUES
& COLOR COOL DRAWINGS!

YUKARI MISHIMA

The Awesome 3-D Art Coloring Guide
First Published in 2020 by Zakka Workshop,
a division of World Book Media, LLC

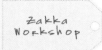

www.zakkaworkshop.com
134 Federal Street
Salem, MA 01970 USA
info@zakkaworkshop.com

TOBIDASU! ODOROKI! TRICK ART (no. 1434)
All rights reserved. Copyright ©2018 Yukari Mishima/Boutique-sha
Originally published in Japanese language by Boutique-Sha, Tokyo, Japan
English language rights, translation & production by World Book Media, LLC
Author: Yukari Mishima
Photography: Hiromu Takeuchi, Yuki Miwa (Studio Dunk)
Design: Momoko Takenaka (Studio Dunk)
Editors: Sakiyo Nitta (Studio Dunk) and Yoh Sasaki
Editorial Supervisor: Ryohei Maruyama
Publisher: Akira Naito
Translator: Mayumi Anzai
English Editor: Kerry Bogert
English Edition Layout: Stacy Wakefield Forte

We have made every effort to ensure the accuracy and completeness of these
instructions. We cannot, however, be responsible for human error, typographical
mistakes, or variations in individual work.

ISBN: 978-1-940552-49-1

Printed in China

10 9 8 7 6 5 4 3 2 1

INTRODUCTION

Welcome to the awesome world of 3-D art!

Learning to take a flat, two-dimensional coloring book drawing and transforming it into a picture that looks like it's popping off the page is both easy and fun. You don't need fancy tools or special materials. With basic colored pencils, scissors, and a couple of my coloring tricks, you'll be creating pictures that you can't wait to show off to your family and friends in no time.

In this coloring book, I'm sharing 20 of my favorite illustrations that are perfect for making 3-D images. Pick your favorite design and follow along, step-by-step, as we make awesome art together.

YUKARI MISHIMA

HOW AWESOME 3-D ART WORKS

An optical illusion is making something appear different from what it really is. In coloring 3-D art, we make flat objects look like they have dimension—making it appear more realistic and lifelike. In this book, we use perspective to trick others into seeing drawings differently. I've already drawn the images for you ahead of time, but here is how it works:

1 Using a basic cylinder as an example, you can see that, looking straight on, it appears balanced. The top is the same size as the bottom, the sides are equal distances apart and the shadows give it some dimension.

2 Now, look at the same image from a different angle. With the drawing on your desk and your new point of view, the top of the cylinder appears to taper and move farther away while the bottom is wider nearest to you. That's perspective!

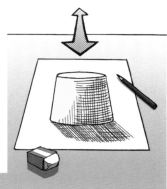

3 We can trick the eye into seeing this cylinder differently by manipulating what we saw change in the perspective. By making the top wider, the sides longer, and the base smaller, we'll achieve an optical illusion.

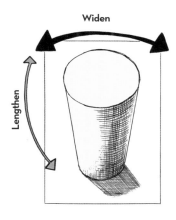

4 When viewed at the same angle as before, the cylinder now looks as if it's sitting on top of the sheet of paper.

5 Removing a portion of the background will take the 3-D effect even further. Simply cut out the area halfway above and behind the cylinder.

6 When taking a photo of your finished 3-D art, add other objects around it and position your light source so the objects cast the same shadow as the drawing.

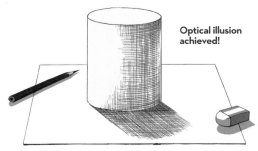

Optical illusion achieved!

WHAT YOU'LL NEED

One of the great things about this 3-D coloring technique is that you don't need a lot of special art supplies. You probably already have everything you need!

ERASER

A simple eraser comes in handy when adding highlights and fixing mistakes.

SHARPENER

Sharp colored pencils are best, so have a standard pencil sharpener nearby.

COLORED PENCILS

A basic set of colored pencils in a full spectrum of colors is a must.

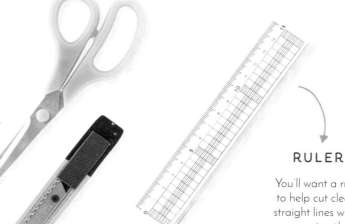

SCISSORS/ UTILITY KNIFE

Scissors are used to remove the background of your picture when you're done coloring. A utility knife will help cut tight, detailed areas.

RULER

You'll want a ruler to help cut clean, straight lines when removing the background.

HOW TO COLOR

With a few basic techniques, simple colors can become more realistic, taking your drawings from good to great. In this book, I guide you through choosing colors for each drawing, but how you hold your pencil and how you layer and blend colors will transform the end result.

HOLD THE PENCIL UPRIGHT

This is the most basic way of coloring on paper. It works best for filling details, getting consistently smooth color, and creating a hard line between two colors.

LAYER AND BLEND COLORS

Drawings become more interesting and complex when colors are layered. It's most effective when using complementary colors and works well when creating an object's shadow.

USE THE SIDE OF THE TIP

When coloring a large area, using the side of the tip can help fill that area more quickly than the tip itself. This technique is also used to create soft textures and to blur edges where color fades away.

SOFTLY LAYER AND BLEND COLORS

Using the side of the tip to layer and blend colors is a great way to create a soft, smooth transition from one color to another—sometimes called a gradient.

3-D COLORING TECHNIQUES

LIGHT SOURCE & SHADOWS

Light and shadow play key roles in achieving a three-dimensional effect in coloring. When light shines on an object, the object blocks the light and casts a shadow. The location of the shadow depends on where the light comes from, or the **light source**. To begin a coloring page, first identify your light source and where the shadows will fall. Don't worry, all the 3-D pictures in this book have step by-step photos and instructions to help with identifying the light source and shadows.

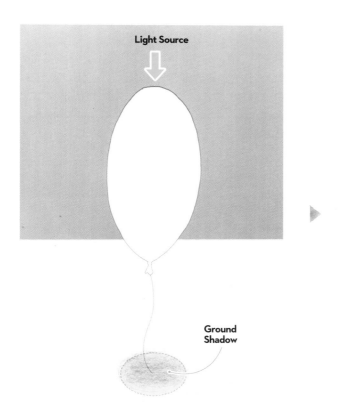

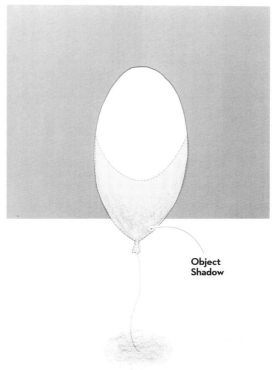

IDENTIFY THE LIGHT SOURCE & CREATE GROUND SHADOW

In this example, imagine the light source is directly above the balloon, causing it to make a round shadow on the ground below. This is called the **ground shadow** and is highlighted in yellow. The shadow will be darkest directly under the balloon and gradually fade away and soften at the edges.

Using gray pencil held at an angle to use the side of the tip, color the round shadow below the balloon so that the shadow is darker in the center and lighter around the outside edge. This is called **shading**. Repeat this step using light blue pencil layered on top of the gray to add more dimension.

CREATE OBJECT SHADOW

The light source will also create a shadow on the object itself. This is called the **object shadow**. Using the same color shading method as the ground shadow, color of the lower half of the balloon with gray and light blue pencils. Use darker shading close to the balloon's knot, which is an area that would be hidden from the light source.

TIP

After you've finished shading, lightly rub the area with a tissue. The tissue will give your shading a smoothly blended look.

STEP

2

COLOR

Once the light source is established and the shadows are added, it's time to color the image. You'll add color with the light source in mind and shade the object to emphasize the three-dimensional effect.

COLOR SHADING

Start to color and shade the balloon using the side of the tip of a pink pencil. Be careful to stay within the outline. Make the balloon appear rounder by applying more pressure when shading the lower half to make it darker and keep the upper half light.

Using a red pencil, apply a layer of red over the pink in the same way.

After coloring, the balloon should appear shaded from very light pink at the top, nearest the light source, to red at the bottom where the object shadow was added.

ADD SHARPNESS

Color the entire balloon with pink pencil again. Then, color over the object shadow again with red pencil to emphasize the shadow. Apply more pressure to the tip of the pencil by holding it upright when coloring around the contours of the balloon. Trace the balloon and its string with a black pencil.

By carefully adding more color to specific areas of the object and outlining it in black, the whole image becomes sharper and more realistic.

MAKE FINAL ADJUSTMENTS

Once you have finished coloring, take a step back and look at the image as a whole. Now's the time to add more color if necessary. Use gray and light blue pencils to add finishing touches to the ground shadow and the balloon's shading. Final adjustments like these are especially important when coloring complex images.

STEP {3}

FINISH

After coloring in the last details of your picture, you're almost ready to share your work. Taking time to add highlights to the brightest areas and cut out the background are two steps you won't want to skip. These simple things go a long way to helping achieve a great optical illusion.

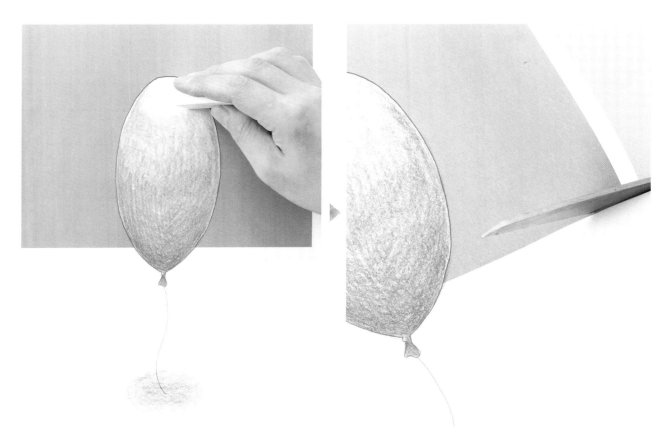

ADD HIGHLIGHTS

Highlights are the brightest areas of an image. You can use an eraser to easily add highlights and further define the light source. The areas to erase will vary based on the image and the light source. For this balloon, lightly rub away the lightest area of color at the very top since the light hits the object from directly above. This will brighten the lightest area near the light source and enhance the 3-D effect.

CUT OUT

The final step is to remove the background. Use scissors to cut away the solid gray area behind the image. For best results, leave a little bit of space around the balloon on your first pass, then go back and trim as close to the image as possible. Cut carefully so that no gray area remains. I recommend using a ruler and utility knife to cut along the straight parts—uneven edges will lessen the 3-D effect.

Erasing too much can cause an unnatural sheen on the paper. Erase gently!

TIP

SHOW OFF YOUR WORK

The final step in this 3-D technique is to take a photo of your work from an angle. When you find just the right angle, elongated areas will appear to be the right size and areas that were tapered or widened will be in proportion.

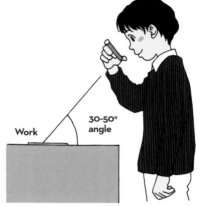

Place the completed work on a level surface. Hold your phone's camera at a 30-50° angle and take a photo. Adjust the angle of your camera as needed to achieve the most realistic perspective.

Coloring **MISTAKES** *to Avoid*

Avoid coloring the ground and object shadows in the same colors as the image itself. The 3-D illusion is more difficult to achieve if colors appear flat.

Avoid coloring outside the lines. Loose coloring will also lessen the 3-D effect.

PLAYFUL PUP

COLORS USED ▶

Gray | Light Blue | Light Brown | Brown | Green | Red | Black | Pink

Light Source

Object Shadow

Ground Shadow

1 Assume that the light is coming from the top left corner. The ground shadows (yellow areas) will appear under the dog's tail and on the ground under the blanket. A large shadow (pink area) appears on the blanket on right side of the dog's body.

2 Color the ground shadows (yellow areas in 1) first. Since the dog and blanket are in contact with the ground, the shadows should be dark and close to the object. Start with gray pencil and add a layer of light blue.

3 Next, color the object shadow (pink area in 1). There is a large shadow on the right side of the dog, and a smaller shadow between the face and blanket, under the ears and chin, and inside the mouth. Again, layer light blue and gray pencils to color the shadow.

4 Color the dog with light brown pencil. The parts of the body in the shadow should be darker while the areas in the light will be brighter. Color the eyes and nose with black pencil and the tongue with pink pencil.

5 Color vertical stripes on the blanket with red pencil, coloring the areas that are exposed to light (the center of the blanket) faintly and the areas in the shadows darker.

6 Color horizontal stripes on the blanket with green pencil. As in step 5, pay attention to the central part of the blanket that is exposed to light and the areas in shadows.

7 Use gray pencil to detail the area where the dog is in contact with the ground. Add a shadow to the tongue to enhance the three-dimensional effect.

8 Use an eraser to add highlights to the dog's nose, the upper half of the front paws, and the upper half of the tail.

9 Cut out the gray area of the background with scissors. Use a utility knife to cut the fine details in the furry tail.

CURIOUS CAT

COLORS USED ▶

Gray   Light Blue   Light Brown   Brown   Pink   Yellow   Light Green   Black

LIGHT SOURCE & SHADOWS

Object Shadow   Light Source

Ground Shadow

1 Assume that the light is directly above the cat. A ground shadow (yellow area) appears on and around the torn paper where the cat is breaking through. Object shadows appear inside the ears, under the face, around the paws, and on the body near the hole (pink areas).

2 First, color the ground shadow (yellow area in 1) by layering gray and light blue pencils. The shadow gets darker as it gets closer to the cat. There is a particularly dark shadow in the hole that is visible over the shoulders of the cat.

3 Next, color the object shadow (pink areas in 1). Focus on the shadows inside the ears, under the face, around the paws, and the areas of the body nearest the hole. Color only the lower half of the front paw to create a three-dimensional effect.

2

COLOR

4 Color the cat with light brown pencil. Leave the fur around the mouth, eyes, and paws white. Layer brown pencil over the light brown in different areas to create furry stripes.

5 Color in the ears, nose, paws, and mouth with pink pencil. Color lightly inside the ears and color the inside of the mouth and the bottom of the nose darker. Color the paws with a gradient, making the bottom half darker and the upper half lighter. This will make the paws appear rounded.

6 Leaving the small oval of each eye white, color the cat's eyes with yellow pencil, and then color the center ovals with black pencil. Finally, use light green pencil to add a ring of green around the black pupils.

3

FINISH

7 Fill in the shadow of the hole with black pencil to show the depth. By coloring the shadow around the hole darker, it will blend in with the other parts.

8 Use an eraser to add highlights to the cat's ears, tip of the nose, and upper half of the front paws.

9 Cut out the gray area of the background. Use a ruler and a utility knife to cut a straight, level line behind the cat.

MAJESTIC CASTLE

COLORS USED ▶

Gray   Light Blue   Blue   Light Brown   Brown   Pink   Black

Object Shadow

Light Source

Ground Shadow

1 Assume that the light is coming from the bottom left. The ground shadows extend to the right and behind the building (yellow areas). Object shadows will appear on the walls of the towers, on the right side of the roof, and behind the windows (pink areas).

2 First, color the ground shadows (yellow areas in 1) with gray and light blue pencils. The shadows at the base of the tower and front entrance are dark with a harsh edge, and the shadows cast by the towers fade and soften at the edges behind the castle.

3 Next, color the object shadows (pink areas in 1). These appear on the walls of the towers that are not exposed to light, on the right side of the roof, behind windows and doorways—where the shadows are darker as you go deeper inside the building.

4 Color the walls of the castle with light brown pencil. Keep in mind that the front wall is closer to the light source and should be colored faintly. The back walls are farther from the light and should be colored darker. Add light brown to the shadows in the windows and doorways, too.

5 Color the tower roofs with light blue and blue pencils. Color the left side where the light hits faintly and the right side darkly. Color the back right tower dome darker on the left to show the shadow created by the central tower.

6 Color the front tower doors with a layer of pink pencil over brown.

7 Use black pencil to add more depth to the windows and doors of the castle.

8 Use an eraser to add highlights to the edge of the castle tower, the dome, and the left side of the front left tower.

9 Cut out the gray area of the background.

Tip: Carefully cut the top of the tower and use clear tape to keep it tacked down, if needed, before photographing.

ICE FISHING

COLORS USED ▶

Gray | Light Blue | Red | Pink | Yellow | Dark Blue | Light Orange | Brown | Light Brown | Black

Light Source

Object Shadow

Ground
Shadow

1   Assume that the light is coming from the back left. The ground shadows appear to the front right of the person, the bucket, and on the back wall of the hole in the ice (yellow areas). The object shadows will appear on the right side of the person and bucket (pink areas).

2   First, color the ground shadows (yellow areas in 1) with gray and light blue pencil. Color the area near the bottom of the wooden box, boots, and bucket darker as they are closer to the ground. Make those shadows lighter as you move away from where the objects are touching the ground.

3   Next, color the object shadows (pink areas in 1) with gray and light blue pencils. The large shadow on the right side of the person, on the right side of the wooden box, and on the right side of the bucket should be darker than the fine shadows on the legs, arms, and head.

4   Color the entire face with light orange pencil. Leave the tip of the nose white, and layer the light orange more heavily under the nose and between the face and hat. Color the cheeks with pink pencil and hair with brown pencil.

5   Have fun coloring the person's clothing with a variety of colors (red, yellow, pink, dark blue, and light brown are shown here). Using the object shadows as your guide, color shaded areas darker and the areas that are exposed to the light source faintly.

6   Color the wooden box with light brown pencil and the bucket with light blue pencil. Again, keep the light source in mind and color light and dark accordingly.

7   Use black pencil to add depth and detail to the darkest areas of the drawing. The bottom of the hole in the ice should be solid black.

8   Use an eraser to add highlights to the top of the hat, the pompom, the edges of the bucket, and the tops of the boots.

9   Cut out the gray area of the background. Use a utility knife to cut the pompom to give it the soft texture of yarn.

FIGURE SKATERS

COLORS USED ▶

Gray   Light   Light   Black   Red   Pink
        Blue   Orange

1

Object Shadow   Ground Shadow

1 Assume that the light is coming from behind and to the left of the skaters. The object shadows appear on their front right side (pink areas). Since the light is coming from the back, a large ground shadow is also created in front of them on the ice (yellow area).

2 First, color the ground shadow (yellow area in 1) with gray and light blue pencils. The shadow should be dark with a crisp edge where the feet meet the ice, and fade as it moves away from there.

3 Next, color the object shadows (pink areas in 1) with gray and light blue pencils. After adding a large shadow on the front side of the bodies (slightly to the right), add detailed shadows that appear under the arms, under the faces, and under the skirt.

2

4 Color the skin with light orange pencil. Leave the parts of the forehead, back of the hands, and fingertips white where they are exposed to the light. Finish the hair with black pencil and the cheeks and mouth with pink and red pencils.

5 Color the clothes with black pencil. Using the shadows as your guide, color the wrinkles darkly. Color shoulders and the area around the knees where the light is shining faintly.

6 Color the flower in the woman's hair and the ruffles of her dress with red pencil. Leave the toes of the skates white.

3

7 If necessary, add more shadow under the face and arms, to the wrinkles in the clothing, and the underside of the ruffles on the woman's skirt.

8 Use an eraser to add highlights to the top of the skaters' heads, the tips of their noses, shoulders, and the toes of the skates to remove the color and give them a glossy look.

9 Cut out the gray area of the background. Use a utility knife to cut the finer details.

SNOWBOARDER

COLORS USED ▶

Gray Light Blue Green Light Light Red Pink
      Blue   Green Orange

LIGHT SOURCE & SHADOWS

Light Source

Ground Shadow

Object Shadow

1 Assume that the light is above and behind the snowboarder, casting a shadow on the snow under him (blue area). Shadows also appear in valleys on the surface of the snow (yellow areas) and on the front of the snowboarder's body (pink area).

2 Layering gray and light blue pencils, color the ground shadows (blue and yellow areas in 1). Color the shadow below the snowboard darker than the valleys in the snow.

3 Continuing with gray and light blue pencils, create the object shadow (pink area in 1) by coloring the front side of the snowboarder's body. Color darker shadows under the face, in the hood, under the arms, and on the snowboard between the feet.

2

COLOR

4 Color the face with light orange pencil. Layer pink pencil on the cheeks under the goggles and use red and pink pencils to color the mouth. Color the hat and goggles with blue pencil, shading the brim and left side of the hat darker. Shade the goggle lens with gray.

5 Color the clothes with green and black pencils. Color under the arms where the object shadow is visible, in the hood, and the wrinkles darker, and the shoulders, back, back of the hands, and calves lighter to emphasize the shadows.

6 Color the entire board with light green pencil. Color between the feet slightly darker to enhance the shadow.

3

FINISH

7 Take special care when finishing the surface of the snow as it is a major part of this image. Smooth out the shading in the valleys by rubbing the surface with a tissue.

8 Add highlights to the snowboard, the back of the gloves, and the tip of the hat by gently erasing color.

9 Cut out the gray area of the background and photograph your work. When taken at an angle of about 30 degrees, the surface of the snow will stand out and maximize the 3-D effect.

SCUBA DIVING

COLORS USED ▶

Gray Light Blue Light Orange Yellow Blue Black Brown

1

LIGHT SOURCE & SHADOWS

Light Source

Object Shadow

Ground Shadow

1 Assume that the light is coming from directly above. A shadow of the diver and the dolphin appears on the seabed (yellow area). The light is hitting their backs, casting large shadows on their stomachs (pink areas).

2 First, color the ground shadow (yellow area in 1) with gray and light blue pencils. Hold the pencils at an angle to create a soft, blurred shadow. Create a gradient so that the center of the shadow is darker and fades toward the outer edges.

3 Next, color the object shadows (pink areas in 1) with gray and light blue pencils. Emphasize the large shadows on the stomachs of the diver and the dolphin. Shadows also appear in the gap between the oxygen tank and the diver's back, and on the underside of the arms and legs.

2

COLOR

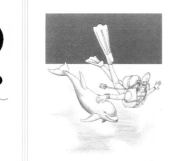

4 Faintly color the entire dolphin with gray pencil. Color over the object shadows on the dolphin's body to deepen the color. Add fine shadows around the eyes, on the underside of the forehead, and on the mouth.

5 Color the diver's face with light orange and the wetsuit with yellow, blue, and black pencils. Darken shadow areas, such as the stomach, arms, legs, goggles, and oxygen tank, to improve the 3-D effect.

6 Color the oxygen tank with gray pencil. Leave the upper half white to show its metallic shine and round shape, and carefully color fine details, such as the goggles and breathing tubes.

3

FINISH

7 Add shadows to the diver's fins and under the hand where it touches the dolphin.

8 Use an eraser to add highlights to the back and forehead of the dolphin, the top of the oxygen tank, the tips of the diver's fins, and the goggle lenses.

9 Carefully cut out the gray area of the background. Use a utility knife to cut out details around the diver's fins.

WONDERFUL WITCH

COLORS USED ▶

Gray   Light Blue   Black   Light Orange   Pink   Red   Light Brown   Brown   Dark Brown

1

LIGHT SOURCE & SHADOWS

Light Source

Object Shadow

Ground Shadow

1 Assume that the light is coming from the upper left. A shadow will appear on the ground under the witch (yellow area). Light strikes the top of her hat, the broom, her knees, arms, and boots, causing shadows to appear over the rest of her body (pink areas).

2 First, color the ground shadow (yellow area in 1) using the side of the tip of gray and light blue pencil. Slightly blur the outline of the ground shadow to show there is a distance between the witch and the ground.

3 Next, add the object shadows (pink areas in 1). Leave the area that is exposed to light white and use gray and light blue pencils to add shadows to other areas, such as the back, hips, and skirt hem.

2

COLOR

4 Color the witch's skin with light orange and her hair with light brown and brown pencils. Add shadows under the chin and nose, and around the face to add dimension. Layer extra brown pencil in her hair to create shadows in the waves. Use pink to color her tongue.

5 Color her clothing and hat with black pencil. The top of the hat that is exposed to light should be colored faintly, and the wrinkles on the clothing in shadows should be colored darkly. Use red pencil to color the rose on her hat and dark brown pencil for her boots.

6 Color the entire broom with light brown pencil. To make the broom handle appear round, color the upper part of the handle lighter and the lower part darker. Add depth to the bristles by layering in more light brown.

3

FINISH

7 Use black pencil to define the details in the shadows. Pay close attention to the areas under the hat, broom, and boots. Shadows in the rose, the ruffles of her dress, and the waves of her hair are also important.

8 Use an eraser to add highlights to the broom handle, top of the hat, tip of the boots, tops of the forearms, and top bristles of the broom.

9 Cut out the gray area of the background.

Tip: Carefully cut the broom handle and tip of the hat. If these areas don't lay flat, use clear tape to tack them down before photographing.

MAGICAL MERMAID

COLORS USED ▶

Gray   *Light Blue*   *Light Orange*   *Pink*   *Yellow*   *Black*   *Blue*   *Green*

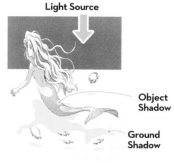

Light Source

Object Shadow

Ground Shadow

1 Assume that the light is coming from directly above. Shadows appear under the mermaid and the fish (yellow areas). The object shadows appear under the mermaid's hair, along the underside of her tail, and under the tail fins of the fish (pink areas).

2 First, color the ground shadows (yellow areas in 1) using the side of the tip of gray and light blue pencils. The outline of the ground shadow should be slightly blurred since there is distance between the mermaid and the ground.

3 Next, color the object shadows (pink areas in 1). Since the light source is directly above, focus on the large shadows that appear on the underside of the body. Shadows also appear under the nose and chin, around the face, and under the arms and hair.

4 Color the upper body of the mermaid with light orange pencil and the hair with gray pencil. Add shadows, layering the colors darker around the back, under the chin and nose, around the face, and in the hair. Color the cheeks with pink pencil.

5 Color the lower body with blue and green pencils. Color the upper side faintly and the lower side darkly to emphasize the shadow.

6 Color the small fish with blue and yellow pencils. Since light is shining from directly above, shadows will appear on the lower halves of the fish. Color the upper halves lightly to show the roundness.

7 Use black pencil to darken the shadows in the mermaid's hair and on the fins of the smallest fish.

8 Use an eraser to highlight the top of the head, the upper half of the arm and the side body of the mermaid, and the upper halves of the fish.

9 Carefully cut out the gray area of the background. Use a utility knife to cut the hair.

Tip: Tack down the strands of floating hair with tape if they curl off the page.

FLYING CARPET

COLORS USED ▶

Gray   Light Blue   Light Orange   Pink   Red   Dark Brown   Black   Violet   Yellow   Dark Blue   Light Brown

Light Source

Object Shadow **Ground Shadow**

1 Assume that the light is coming from directly above. A large ground shadow will appear under the flying carpet (yellow area). The object shadows are created where the children and the carpet meet, on the boy's legs, and the front of the girl's body (pink areas).

2 First, color the ground shadow (yellow area in 1) using the side of the tip of gray and light blue pencils. The outline of the ground shadow should be slightly blurred as there is a distance between the carpet and the ground.

3 Next, add the object shadows (pink areas in 1). There is a particularly dark shadow where the carpet is in contact with the children's bodies. It's also important to pay attention to the shadow of the boy's arm extending downward along the curved surface of the carpet.

4 Color the children's skin with light orange pencil. Layer additional color around the edges of the faces, under the noses and chins, and along the girl's lower legs. Add shadow to the indented areas of the boy's body, such as under the toes, under the heel, and between the fingers.

5 Color the children's clothes with yellow, red, and dark blue pencils. Color the boy's shoulders to thighs and the girl's shoulders and knees faintly where the light shines on them.

6 Color the carpet with yellow, dark brown, and violet pencils. Color light shades first, and then add dark colors to create depth.

7 Use black pencil to color the shadow behind the wavy carpet deeply.

8 Use an eraser to add highlights to the high points of the folds in the carpet, the children's shoulders, the top of the girl's foot, and the top of the boy's hand.

9 Carefully cut out the gray area of the background. Use a ruler to make sure the line behind the carpet is straight.

A ROSE IN BLOOM

COLORS USED ▶

Gray   Light   Red   Light   Light   Pink   Brown   Green
       Blue   Green   Orange

1

LIGHT SOURCE & SHADOWS

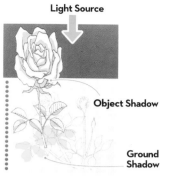

Light Source

Object Shadow

Ground Shadow

1   In this illusion, you'll make it look as if a real rose is growing out of a sheet of paper containing a sketch of roses. Assume that the light is coming from directly above. The ground shadow will appear directly under the 3-D rose (yellow area). The object shadows appear in the layers of the petals and on the leaves (pink areas).

2   First, color the ground shadow (yellow area in 1) using the side of the tip of gray and light blue pencils. Darken the shadow as it gets closer to the stem of the rose.

3   Next, color the object shadows (pink areas in 1) with gray and light blue. Dark shadows appear in the layers of overlapping petals, on the leaves, and on the stem just below the flower.

2

COLOR

4   Color the sketch of the rose roughly and without any shadow to make it appear flat. Use red for flowers, green for leaves, and light green and orange for stems.

5   Color the 3-D rose with pink pencil, then add red over the shadowed areas of the petals. Add extra dimension to the petals by drawing short red lines in the direction the petal is growing.

6   Color the leaves of the 3-D rose light green and green, and the stems light green and orange.

3

FINISH

7   Add subtle accents of red to the tips of the thorns to make them look more realistic.

8   Use an eraser to add highlights to the petals and the tips of the leaves.

9   Cut out the gray area of the background.

Tip: Use a hole punch to cut out the round holes along the left side of the image. Then tear each hole to the edge to make it look like it's been ripped from a sketchbook.

HOT AIR BALLOONS

COLORS USED ▶

Gray   Light Blue   Blue   Yellow   Black   Light Green   Red   Orange   Pink   Green   Violet   Purple   Brown

Light Source

Object Shadow   Ground Shadow

1 Assume that the light is coming from directly above. A round shadow will appear on the ground just below each balloon (yellow areas). The object shadows appear on lower half of the balloons (pink areas).

2 First, color the ground shadows (yellow areas in 1) using the side of the tip of gray and light blue pencils. Since there is distance between the balloon and the ground, the outline of the ground shadow is slightly blurred with darker color concentrated in the center.

3 Next, color the object shadows (pink areas in 1) with gray and light blue pencils. Since the light hits from directly above, focus on the bottom half. Make a gradient with the darkest shading at the base of the balloon and fade up to the lightest shade.

4 Use your favorite pencils to color the left balloon. Color it carefully and evenly by holding the colored pencil upright. Color the basket at the base of the balloon with brown.

5 Next, color the center balloon with your favorite pencils. As in step 4, color carefully and evenly with the tip of the pencils. Color the basket brown, but layer extra color so it appears slightly darker.

6 Then, use your favorite pencils to color the right balloon. Add colors in the same way as in steps 4 and 5. Color the basket brown.

7 Color the people viewing from the ground with a sharp blue pencil. Since they're small and should look as if they're far below the balloons, they don't have much detail. Color their shadows in the same style.

8 Use an eraser to highlight the top of each balloon where the light source casts the brightest light.

9 Cut out the gray area of the background. If needed, use a ruler and utility knife to cut a level horizon line.

SOARING PARROT

COLORS USED ▶

Gray   Light   Blue   Yellow   Black   Light
        Blue   Green

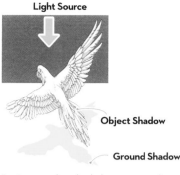

Light Source

Object Shadow

Ground Shadow

1 Assume that the light is coming from directly above. A shadow will appear on the ground just below the bird (yellow area). Object shadows appear on the bird's body, at the base of the wings, and where the feathers overlap (pink areas).

2 First, color the ground shadow (yellow area in 1) with the side of the tip of gray and light blue pencils. The outer edge of the ground shadow is slightly blurred as there is a distance between the bird and the ground.

3 Next, color the object shadows (pink areas in 1) with gray and light blue pencils. Triangular shadows will appear on the bird's body at the base of the wings (blue areas). Add darker shadows in these areas and to the underside of the tail feathers, to give it a more realistic 3-D feel.

4 Color the whole bird with light blue pencil, but leave the face and eye area white.

5 Color the bird's wings with blue pencil. Carefully add color to each wing. Color the part of the wing where the light hits faintly, and color the base darker where the shadows appear.

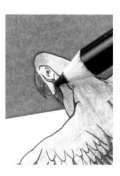

6 Color the details around the face and head with light green, black, and yellow pencils.

7 Add extra depth to the wings with added layers of gray and blue as appropriate to enhance the shadow.

8 Use an eraser to add highlights where the light hits the back, head, and wings.

9 Cut out the gray area of the background. Cut the detailed area of the wings with a utility knife. Tack the feathers down with tape if needed.

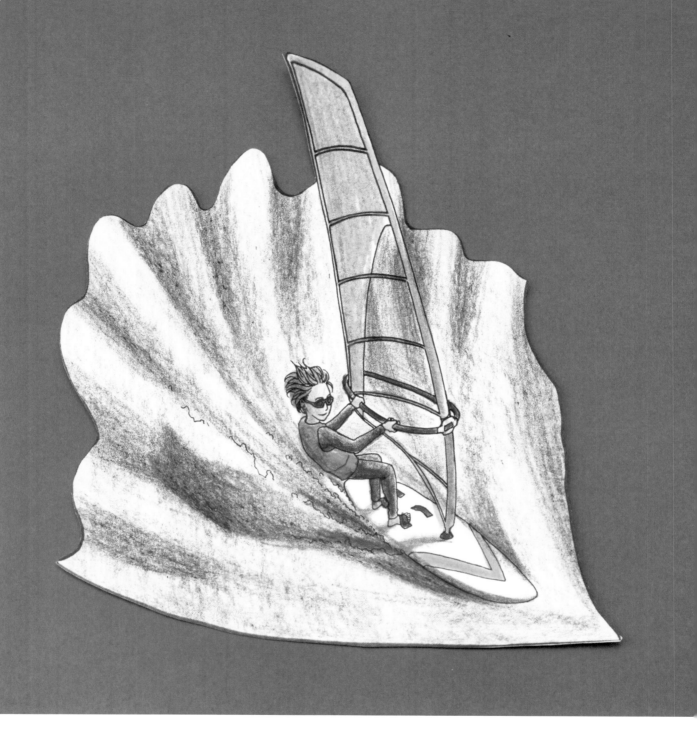

WINDSURFING

COLORS USED ▶

Gray   Light Blue   Light Orange   Yellow   Brown   Black   Orange   Blue

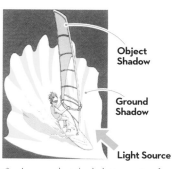

Object
Shadow

Ground
Shadow

Light Source

1 Assume that the light is coming from the lower right, in front of the surfer. A reflection of the sail extends from the board to the left rear on the surface of the water (light blue area). Object shadows also appear on the back of the sail and the surfer (pink areas). The ground shadows (yellow areas) appear in the ripples of the waves.

2 First, color the ground shadows (yellow areas in 1) with gray and light blue pencils. Enhance the waves by creating a gradient from light to dark in each ripple. Color the shadows of the waves that can be seen through the transparent sail too.

3 Next, color the object shadows (pink areas in 1) with gray and light blue pencil. Do not color the transparent area of the sail. Color the shadows on the surfer's back and feet.

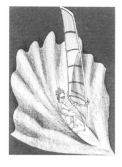

4 Color the waves with blue pencil. Since the area is large, it is important to color using the side of the tip. Color over the entire area several times to enhance the depth of color in the shadows.

5 Color the surfer's skin with light orange pencil. Color the left half of the face darkly. Color the wetsuit with orange and black. Emphasize the shadows on the back, under the arms, and behind the thighs with extra layers of color.

6 Color the entire sail with yellow pencil. Use black pencil to add a shadow that extends from the feet of the surfer and the base of the sail, across the board toward the left rear.

7 Darken the sail's reflection on the water by lightly coloring a layer of black in that area.

8 Use an eraser to add highlights to the crests of the waves.

9 Carefully cut out the gray area of the background before photographing.

TROPICAL FISH

COLORS USED ▶

Gray   Light Blue   Black   Yellow   Orange   Blue   Brown

1

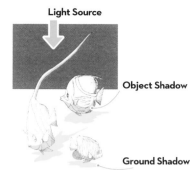

Light Source

Object Shadow

Ground Shadow

1 Assume that the light is coming from directly above the fish. A shadow will appear on the ground just below each fish (yellow areas). The object shadows appear on the undersides of the bellies and the bottoms of the tail fins (pink areas).

2 First, color the ground shadows (yellow areas in 1) using the side of the tip of gray and light blue pencils. Blur the outer edge of the ground shadow slightly as there is distance between the fish and the ground.

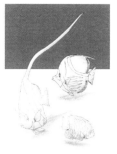

3 Next, color the object shadows (pink areas in 1) with gray and light blue pencils. Since the light hits from directly above, emphasize the lower half of each fish by coloring it darker.

2

COLOR

4 Color the fish on the left with your favorite pencils. Start with a light color and then add darker colors on top. Remember, the color should become heavier as it moves down the body to emphasize the lighting.

5 Color the fish in the back with your favorite pencils. Add a little color to the tail fin with light blue pencil to create a cool and transparent feeling.

6 Color the fish in front with your favorite pencils. Since the pattern on this fish is more detailed, use a sharp tip to color the areas carefully.

3

FINISH

7 Add a shadow to the lower half of the long top fin of the left fish to create a more three-dimensional effect.

8 Use an eraser to add highlights to the top of each fish. These subtle bright spots make the shadows more effective.

9 Cut out the gray area of the background carefully.

Tip: Use clear tape to tack down the long fin of the left fish, if needed.

SECRET STAIRCASE

COLORS USED ▶

Gray *Light Blue* *Light Brown* *Brown* *Black* *Light Orange* *Dark Brown* *Green* *Yellow* *Dark Blue*

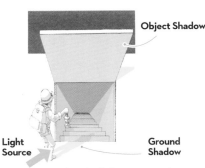

Object Shadow

Light
Source

Ground
Shadow

1 Assume that the light is coming from the bottom left. A ground shadow extends from the feet and stairwell door, toward the right rear (yellow area). Object shadows appear in front of the explorer, under the backpack, and inside the door (pink area).

2 First, color the ground shadow (yellow area in 1). The shadow extending from the explorer should be clearly defined in the outline of a person. The shadow should be darkest along the back of the stairwell—color over this area several times to increase the depth.

3 Next, color the object shadows (pink areas in 1). The door of the stairwell has a large shadow on the entire vertical surface. Leave the horizontal surface along the top of the door white.

4 Color the stairs with light brown pencil. Hold the pencil straight up and down and apply heavy pressure to achieve a solid dark color in the stairwell. Layer black pencil over the light brown to create a gradient effect on the side walls.

5 Color the door with brown pencil. It is important to differentiate the horizontal surface that is exposed to light and the vertical surface that is shaded. The horizontal surface should be lighter.

6 Use light orange, light brown, green, black, and brown pencil to color the explorer's skin, clothing, backpack, and lantern. Color over the object shadows to create more depth and dimension.

7 Color the back of the stairwell until it is completely black, and color over it with dark blue pencil.

8 Erase the area around the lantern to create a softly lit effect. Add highlights to other areas by lightly erasing the top of the hat, the front side of the backpack, and the horizontal surface of the door.

9 Carefully cut out the gray area of the background. This image features straight lines, so use a ruler and utility knife to achieve the best effect.

GERBERA DAISIES

COLORS USED ▶

Gray · Light Blue · Brown · Yellow · Orange · Dark Brown · Red · Green · Light Green · Blue

1

LIGHT SOURCE & SHADOWS

Light Source

Object Shadow

Ground Shadow

1 Assume that the light is coming from the top left. A shadow extends from the base of the daisies to the right rear (yellow area), and object shadows also appear on the back of the petals and on the stem just below the flowers (pink areas).

2 First, color the ground shadow (yellow area in 1) using the side of the tip of gray and light blue pencils. The coloring should be darker as you get closer to the cluster of leaves.

3 Next, color the object shadows (pink areas in 1) with gray and light blue. Shadows will be darker where petals and leaves overlap, and on the stems just below the flowers.

2

COLOR

4 Color the circular base with brown pencil. Color heavier in the shadowed areas of the ground to emphasize the shadow under the leaves.

5 Color the petals with orange pencil. The color should be darker toward the center where the petals meet and overlap and lighter toward the tips where the petals are exposed to light. Layer red pencil over the orange to deepen the color of the petals.

6 Color the stems and leaves with light green pencil. Leave the edges of the leaves a little lighter. Add green pencil on top to emphasize the shadows around the veins and create a three-dimensional effect.

3

FINISH

7 Add more dimension to the dark shadows by adding a layer of blue pencil.

8 Use an eraser to add highlights to the tips of the petals and edges of the leaves.

9 Cut out the gray area of the background.

Tip: If the petals are floating, use tape to tack them down before photographing.

GERBERA DAISIES ～ 47

EARTH AND MOON

COLORS USED ▶

Gray   *Light Blue*   *Blue*   *Yellow*   *Orange*

1

LIGHT SOURCE & SHADOWS

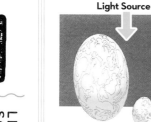

Light Source

Object Shadow

Ground Shadow

1 Assume that the light is coming from directly above. Shadows will appear on the ground just below the Earth and moon (yellow areas). The object shadows appear on the lower portion of each sphere (pink areas).

2 First, color the ground shadows (yellow areas in 1) using the side of the tip of gray and light blue pencils. The outer edges of the shadows should be blurred as there is distance between the spheres and the ground.

3 Next, color the object shadows. Since the light is shining from directly above, a shadow shaped like a crescent appears on the lower half of each sphere (blue areas). Using gray and light blue pencils, color a gradient that is darker at the bottom and lighter at the top of the crescent.

2

COLOR

4 Color the Earth with blue pencil, leaving the narrow cloud areas white.

5 Color the moon with yellow pencil.

6 Color the details of the moon's surface with a sharp orange pencil.

3

FINISH

7 Enhance the shadows, layering more gray and light blue pencil. Darken the center of ground shadow to maximize the floating effect.

8 Use an eraser to add a highlight to the top of each sphere, being careful not to remove too much color.

9 Cut out the gray area of the background. Because this image features spheres, it is more noticeable if the lines are not cut smoothly. So, cut carefully.

BUTTERFLIES

COLORS USED ▶

Gray *Light Blue* *Brown* *Dark Brown* *Black*

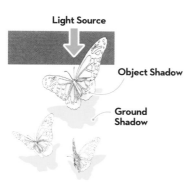

Light Source

Object Shadow

Ground
Shadow

1 Assume that the light is coming from directly above. Shadows appear on the ground directly below the butterflies (yellow areas). In addition, light shadows appear from the base of the wings toward the tips (pink areas).

2 First, color the ground shadows (yellow areas in 1) using the side of the tip of gray and light blue pencils. The outer edges of the shadows should be blurred as there is distance between the butterflies and the ground.

3 Next, color the object shadows (pink areas in 1). Add shadows to the back of the wing of the lower right butterfly. Also, lightly shade the bodies of the butterflies from the base of the wings toward the tips.

4 Color the wings of each butterfly with light blue pencil. Fill the wings completely, shading the areas closest to the body darker than the tips.

5 Using a sharp brown pencil, color the pattern on the lower portion of the wings. Again, keeping the light source in mind, concentrate darker color toward the body while keeping the outer edges of the wings lighter.

6 Using a sharp black pencil, color the pattern on the upper portion of the wings. Also color the bodies of the butterflies with black pencil.

7 Check that the details of the body pattern on each butterfly wing have been fully colored. Add additional shading as needed.

8 Erase any areas of color that travel outside the lines of the butterflies' wings.

9 Cut out the gray area of the background and photograph your work. Adjust the angle of the camera as necessary to achieve the best 3-D effect.

DRAGON

This final drawing has a unique approach.
You'll color it and then fold it in half for the final effect.

COLORS USED ▶

Gray   Light   Brown   Light   Pink   Red   Blue   Yellow   Green   Light   Black
       Blue   Orange   Green

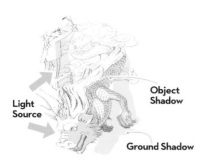

Light
Source

Object
Shadow

Ground Shadow

1 Assume that the light is coming from the left side. Shadows of the girl and the dragon appear on the wall and ground (yellow areas). The object shadows appear on the front of the girl's body and the side of the dragon's stomach (pink areas).

2 First, color the ground shadows (yellow areas in 1) with gray and light blue pencils. Color the shadow of the wall where the dragon is popping out especially dark, and then blur the outer edges of the shadow slightly.

3 Next, color the object shadows (pink areas in 1) with gray and light blue pencils. Pay close attention to the shape of the shadow on the dragon's face.

4 Color the girl's skin, hair, and clothes. The back side is exposed to light, so it should be bright, while the wall side should be darker from the shadows. Soft shadows also appear under the nose and chin, under the arms, and under the apron.

5 Color the dragon's body, layering light green and green pencils. Color the area closest to the wall and the ground darker. Color the mouth red, the eyes yellow, and the horns brown. Leave the forehead, eyebrows, and nose wrinkles white.

6 Color part of the wall mural with green pencil. To make the dragon's three-dimensional effect stand out, color the wall mural roughly and without shadows so it appears flat. Color the stool and paintbrush.

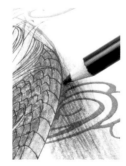

7 Use black pencil to color a shadow beneath the dragon's body where it pops out of the wall. Add lighter layers of black to the dragon's mouth, nostrils, and claws.

8 Use an eraser to highlight the dragon's eyebrows, nose, and horns, and the back of the girl's head.

9 You don't need to cut anything out for this drawing. Instead, fold it in half at the center and prop it up at a right angle. Photograph the image from the upper right corner of the work. You'll know you've achieved the optical illusion when the dragon appears parallel to the tabletop.

3-D ART COLORING PAGES

To start coloring your own awesome 3-D art, cut out your favorite drawing from this section and follow the instructions provided.

COLORING INSTRUCTIONS ON PAGE 15

COLORING INSTRUCTIONS
ON PAGE 19

COLORING INSTRUCTIONS ON PAGE 21

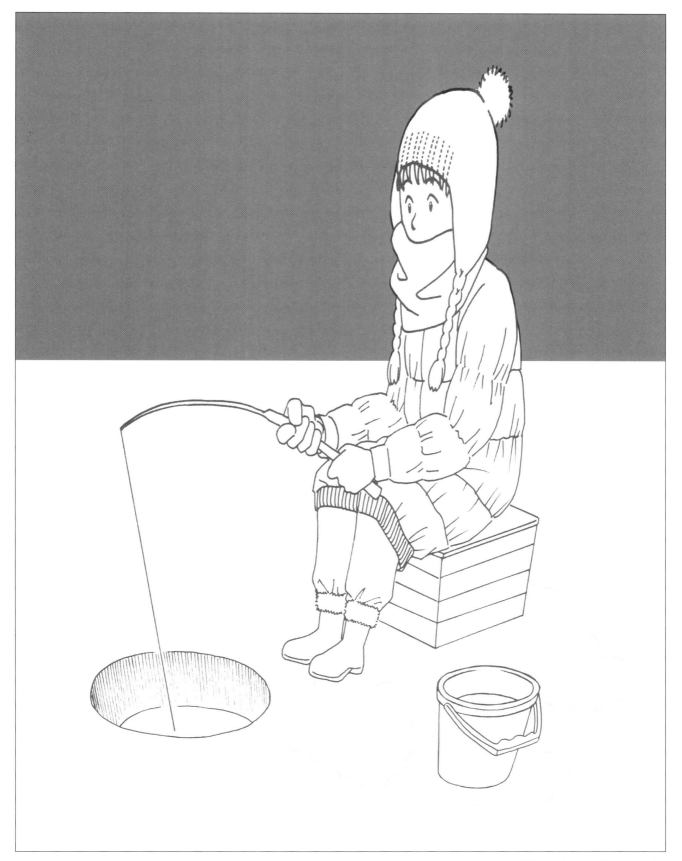

№ 5 FIGURE SKATERS

COLORING INSTRUCTIONS
ON PAGE 23

COLORING INSTRUCTIONS
ON PAGE 25

COLORING INSTRUCTIONS ON PAGE 27

COLORING INSTRUCTIONS
ON PAGE 29

COLORING INSTRUCTIONS
ON PAGE 31

COLORING INSTRUCTIONS
ON PAGE 33

COLORING INSTRUCTIONS
ON PAGE 35

COLORING INSTRUCTIONS
ON PAGE 37

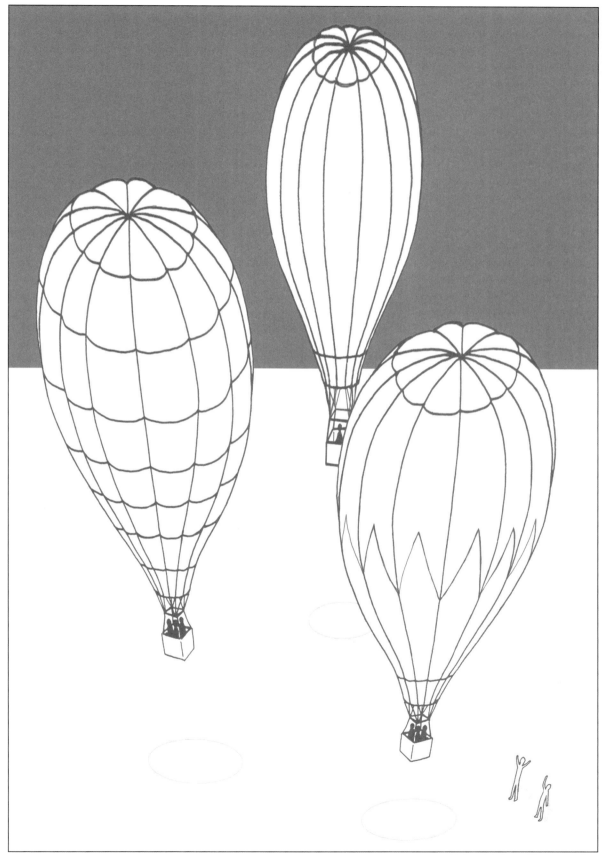

COLORING INSTRUCTIONS ON PAGE 41

COLORING INSTRUCTIONS
ON PAGE 43

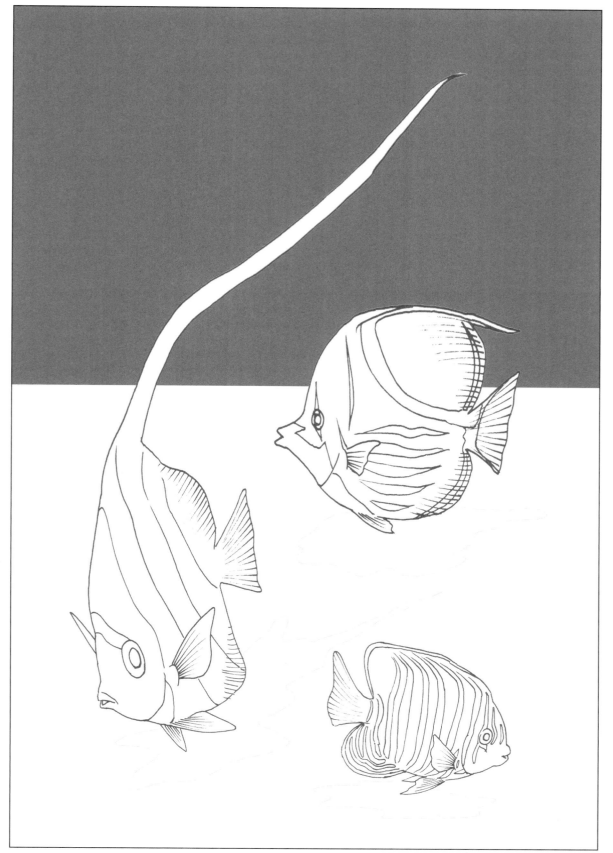

№ 16 SECRET STAIRCASE

COLORING INSTRUCTIONS
ON PAGE 45

№ 19 BUTTERFLIES

COLORING INSTRUCTIONS ON PAGE 51

COLORING INSTRUCTIONS ON PAGE 53

SHARE YOUR WORK
ON SOCIAL MEDIA!

Don't forget to photograph your amazing 3-D art
and share it on social media!

We'd love to see your finished artwork! You can
use the following hashtag or make up your own:

#3Dartcoloring

ABOUT THE AUTHOR

Yukari Mishima was born in 1980. After majoring in Chinese in college, Yukari began working as a translator and proofreader. During this time, she continued exploring her love for illustration and participated in various art competitions. In 2015, Yukari began working as a freelance illustrator and has created artwork for multiple books published in Japan.